This book is dedicated to all beings who have enjoyed the splendor of The Park. May we continue to care for it in a way that provides opportunity for generations to come.

From the Author:

I'd like to offer gratitude to all of the partners and students who I've spent time with in the mountains. Thank you for being a part of my journey! Thanks to Mark Kelly and a plug for his book: Backcountry Skiing and Ski Mountaineering in Rocky Mountain National Park. This was the first book of its kind for RMNP and was a monumental effort. Mark has also been a tremendous resource for all things Park skiing during his tenure in Estes. Finally, thanks to Andy Sovick for keeping me on track throughout this process, and to all of my colleagues and peers of ski touring and ski mountaineering who helped to make this book possible.

From the publisher:

Without our team of incredible specialists, these books and maps would not be possible. Graphic design by Keitha Kostyk, aerial images by Alex Neuschaefer (Summit Aerial Media), cartography by Farid Tabian (Singletrack Maps), and editing by Emma Walker. Fact checking and "responsibility review" by some of the most accomplished and reliable ski mountaineers in the park.

About the Author: Mike Soucy, IFMGA Mountain Guide

Mike Soucy is a lifelong skier and avid climber who has frequented Rocky Mountain National Park for 25 years. Winter and spring often find him searching for sheltered powder turns, exploring the lesser-visited corners of the Park, or just taking a quick lap at Hidden Valley. For Mike, summer and fall are for rock and alpine climbing on the walls that form the scenic backdrop for his favorite ski descents.

No matter the season, Mike earns a living working as a local mountain guide. The Park is often the training ground where he and his guests prepare for trips to the Alaska Range, Canadian Rockies, or European Alps. Mike strives to be a reliable resource for route beta and conditions, as well as a trusted partner and mentor to his friends and students in the mountains.

Get the book and map on your
Downloadable for offline use, each of
is available in digital form. With the c
button, you get access to GPS naviga
our aerial photos, route descriptions,
and more. Shop for your digital guide
here on the Beacon Guidebooks webs

© Beacon Guidebooks 2022
Published by Beacon Guidebooks, Gunnison, Colorado

Cover 📷 Fred Marmsater   **Aerials** 📷 Summit Aerial Media   **Additional** 📷 Alex Buis

BACKCOUNTRY SKIING ETHICS + BEST PRACTICES

The growing popularity of backcountry skiing in Colorado has exceeded all prior expectations. Skills and behaviors that were once assumed to take years to develop are now expected immediately of new-to-the-sport backcountry skiers and riders. To better understand these community expectations please review these ethics and best practices for the safety and enjoyment of all users.

Leave No Trace Seven Principles

1. Plan Ahead and Prepare
2. Travel and Camp on Durable Surfaces
3. Dispose of Waste Properly
4. Leave What You Find
5. Minimize Campfire Impacts
6. Respect Wildlife
7. Be Considerate of Other Visitors

© Leave No Trace: www.LNT.org

Setting and Using Skintracks

This atlas includes commonly used approaches for each sector, but conditions and circumstances may dictate other options. Knowing good etiquette for setting community-minded skintracks minimizes user conflict.

✔ Set skintracks with an eye to safety and the lowest possible risk
✔ Avoid unnecessarily steep terrain or multiple switchbacks
✔ Keep skintracks off the slopes being skied or ridden down
✔ Never walk or snowshoe on a ski skintrack
✔ Step aside to allow faster skiers to pass you

Preparing for a Backcountry Ski Trip

Effective planning for a backcountry skiing day involves aspects of safety, comfort, and communication. Allow every member of your party to have an equal part in determining routes, safety, and risk tolerance.

✔ Read the daily weather and avalanche report before arriving at the trailhead
✔ Compare the avalanche report to the terrain you plan to ski or ride
✔ Confirm your party has the appropriate safety gear (beacon, probe, shovel) and the knowledge to properly use it
✔ Consider the use of advanced safety gear: avalanche airbag, radios, and GPS devices
✔ Check that your party has appropriate over-the-snow travel gear for the intended terrain
✔ Ensure that adequate clothing, accessories, food, and water is carried by each party member

Dogs and Backcountry Skiing

Dogs are prohibited in the National Park, but we're putting this information in here anyway for those who will also be skiing elsewhere with Fido. Few issues can provoke more strong opinions than taking dogs on backcountry ski trips. Regardless of your decision whether or not to bring a dog, consider the ramifications to all users.

✔ Do not put an avalanche beacon on your dog that has the same radio frequency as human-worn beacons
✔ Dogs should always be under full leash or voice control to avoid entering avalanche terrain and to prevent user conflict
✔ Provide full pet first aid, winter injury care, food, and water for your dog
✔ Be prepared with the knowledge and equipment to evacuate your dog if necessary

TABLE OF CONTENTS

USEFUL TOOLS IN THIS GUIDE

Our graphics are designed to give you a quick reference to some of the key elements in your decision-making process.

General Aspect
The general direction all runs in a particular zone will face.

ATES Ratings
We label and color all zones and descents according to their ATES ratings. *See page 9* to learn more about ATES.

Max Slope Angle / Descent Elevation Loss

Ascent Line

Descent Line

Ascend / Descend

Objective Hazard

Avalanche Terrain Information

Parking / Trailhead / Skintrack Start

Access / Ascent / Skintrack Information

Exit Information

Parking Lot / Area

EVERY LOCATION IN THIS ATLAS IS PRIME AVALANCHE TERRAIN.

Every location in this book is prime avalanche terrain. The terrain in "The Park" backcountry is steep with varying levels of exposure to avalanche activity. Beacon Guidebooks uses the ATES rating system to help readers understand that variation and choose tours that match the risk described in the CAIC daily avalanche forecast. This book is only one of many tools that can help skiers and riders make better plans and decisions for backcountry travel. Nevertheless, backcountry travel is inherently dangerous. Use these tools and ski/ride at your own risk.

Avalanche safety is extremely important for anyone recreating in the mountains of Colorado.

GET THE FORECAST

ROCKY MOUNTAIN NATIONAL PARK ROAD INFO

KNOW THE CDOT ROAD CONDITIONS

NORTH AMERICAN AVALANCHE DANGER SCALE

EXTREME
Avoid all avalanche terrain.

HIGH
Very dangerous avalanche conditions. Travel in avalanche terrain not recommended.

CONSIDERABLE
Dangerous avalanche conditions. Careful snowpack evaluation, cautious route-finding and conservative decision making are essential.

MODERATE
Heightened avalanche conditions on specific terrain features. Evaluate snow and terrain carefully; identify features of concern.

LOW
Generally safe avalanche conditions. Watch for unstable snow on isolated terrain features.

NO RATING
Watch for signs of unstable snow such as recent avalanches, cracking in the snow and audible collapsing. Avoid traveling on or under similar slopes.

ALL BEACON GUIDEBOOKS MAPS AND ATLASES USE THE ATES SYSTEM.

ATES (Avalanche Terrain Exposure Scale) is a planning tool designed and used extensively in Canada. It helps identify appropriate terrain for the avalanche hazard of the day, but it does not predict the stability of a given slope. *Source: Government of Canada. Parks Canada. pc.gc.ca/en.*

Our authors characterize and classify the terrain of each sector of their backcountry zone. Once classified, we fit them into one of three categories: 1-Simple, 2-Challenging, or 3-Complex. The definitions are below. These green, blue, and black, colors should not be confused with the difficulty of a run (like we are used to seeing in a ski resort). Green means: Simple avalanche terrain. Blue means: Challenging avalanche terrain. Black means: Complex avalanche terrain.

SIMPLE ZONES
Exposure to low angle or primarily forested terrain. Some forest openings may involve the runout zones of infrequent avalanches and terrain traps may exist. Many options to reduce or eliminate exposure.

SIMPLE ROUTES
offer options to reduce your exposure to avalanche terrain in Challenging zones.

CHALLENGING ZONES
Exposure to well defined avalanche paths, starting zones, terrain traps or overhead hazard. Options exist to reduce or eliminate exposure with careful routefinding.

CHALLENGING ROUTES
offer options to reduce your exposure to avalanche terrain in Complex zones.

COMPLEX ZONES
Exposure to multiple overlapping avalanche paths or large expanses of steep, open terrain. Sustained exposure to overhead hazard. Many avalanche starting zones and terrain traps with minimal options to reduce exposure.

CHALLENGING ROUTES
increase your exposure to higher consequence avalanche terrain.

Study the terrain in this book and on our topo map. Understand how it relates to the ATES scale, and what kind of objective hazards each tour might be exposed to.

Get the avalanche forecast. Then, using the Avaluator, connect the avalanche danger rating with the terrain rating of the area you plan on visiting to provide a recommendation on what level of caution should be taken given the forecasted avalanche conditions. You can then decide whether or not to proceed or go somewhere else.

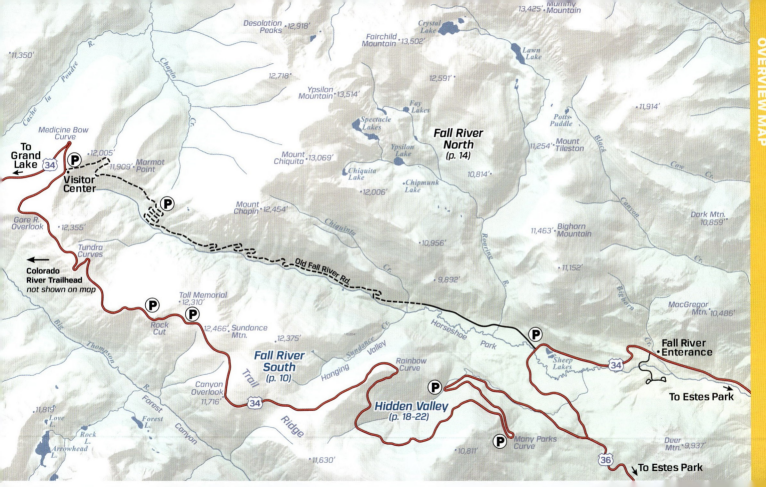

'11,350'

Cache la Poudre R.

Chapin Cr.

Desolation Peaks '12,918'

Fairchild Mountain 13,502'

Crystal Lake

13,425' Mummy Mountain

Lawn Lake

Medicine Bow Curve

To Grand Lake
34

'12,005'

Marmot Point

11,909'

12,718'

Ypsilon Mountain 13,514'

Fay Lakes

12,591'

'11,914'

Potts Puddle

Mount Tileston

Visitor Center

Spectacle Lakes

Ypsilon Lake

Fall River North (p. 14)

11,254'

Black Canyon

Gore R. Overlook

'12,355'

Tundra Curves

Mount Chiquita '13,069'

Chiquita Lake

Chipmunk Lake

10,814'

11,463' Bighorn Mountain

Dark Mtn. 10,859'

Mount Chapin '12,454'

'12,006'

Colorado River Trailhead not shown on map

Chiquinta Cr.

'10,956'

Roaring R.

'11,152'

Toll Memorial '12,310'

34

12,466' Sundance Mtn.

'9,892'

MacGregor Mtn. '10,486'

Rock Cut

Big Thompson R.

Canyon Overlook 11,716'

34

'12,375'

Hanging Valley

Sundance Cr.

Trail Ridge

Rainbow Curve

Horseshoe Park

Sheep Lakes

34

Fall River Enterance

To Estes Park

Fall River South (p. 10)

Hidden Valley (p. 18-22)

Many Parks Curve

'11,819' Love L.

Rock L. Arrowhead L.

Forest L.

Forest Canyon

'11,630'

'10,811'

36

Deer Mtn. '9,937'

To Estes Park

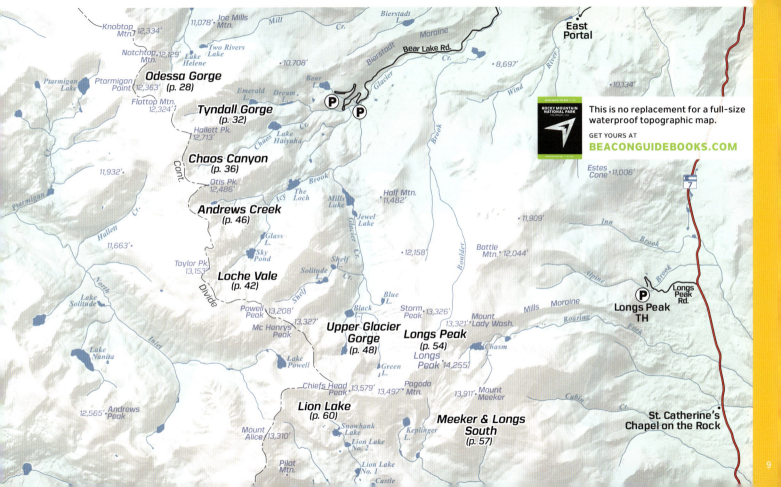

Never Summer Range

Trail Ridge

Trail Ridge Road

Fall River

FALL RIVER SOUTH

On the south side of Fall River lies Sundance Mountain. With the exception of Hanging Valley, its north and east slopes are most commonly accessed in late spring, after the opening of Trail Ridge Road. Midwinter adventure is accessed via Hidden Valley. Sundance's North Face offers a long, sustained fall line that often holds snow well into June. The Northeast Couloirs are shorter excursions that require a hike back out to your vehicle on Trail Ridge. Old Fall River Road usually opens to vehicles around the beginning of July, often too late for bottom-up or car shuttle excursions. However, the April 1 opening for bicycles offers some room for creativity.

The leeward position of this terrain in the alpine often lends itself to wind slab avalanches in the winter and into mid-spring. By the time Trail Ridge Road opens, wet snow avalanche problems become a greater concern.

For Hanging Valley Bowl, midwinter access is up and over Hidden Valley's Upper Main run. This adds a nice extension onto a typical HV tour. In the spring, parking is available right on top of it at the Ute Trailhead. Sundance's North Face and Northeast Couloirs are accessed from above, via pullouts on Trail Ridge Rd.

Approaching these lines often requires walking over tundra to the leeward aspects of Sundance Mountain. Please follow trails whenever possible, or disperse your group to minimize impact on the fragile vegetation.

In the springtime, the most common exit strategy is to simply reverse your route back to the car. Sundance's North Face, and occasionally the Northeast Couloirs, will fill in all the way down to Fall River. This requires a climb back out or a shuttle vehicle placed at the road closure.

❶ HANGING VALLEY 35° 600'

Hanging Valley provides a secluded bowl on the leeward side of Trail Ridge, just north of Hidden Valley. To access it in the winter, climb up and over the top of the Upper Main Slope and descend north (sometimes on foot) to Trail Ridge Road. The north-facing aspect of the bowl has sparse trees and <30° skiing. The east-facing aspect opens up and exceeds 30° as it drops into Sundance Creek. To exit, return to Hidden Valley. Hanging Valley often holds snow into June. When the road opens in spring, parking is available at its top, at the Ute Trailhead.

❷ SUNDANCE NORTH FACE 40° 2,000'

A Trail Ridge springtime classic. This top-down run begins just north of the Toll Memorial. Park at the Rock Cut and use the trail to approach. Ski as far down as you're willing to climb back up. It gets steeper as you go…

❸ SUNDANCE NORTHEAST COULOIRS 50° 1,200'

Another one best accessed after the road opens in the spring. Use the pullouts east of the Rock Cut and walk across tundra towards Sundance Mountain's summit. Two couloirs drop cleanly from the ridge just north of the summit and provide fun steep turns to the talus. Boot back out.

EXIT

Trail Ridge Road

Mount Richthofen

Mount Chapin

EXIT

See next pages for: ③ Y LEFT ④ CUMBRE COULOIR ⑤ FAIRCHILD SOUTH FACE

FALL RIVER NORTH

To the north of Fall River, you'll find classic ski mountaineering objectives off the Mummy Range summits of Mount Chiquita, Ypsilon Mountain, and Fairchild Mountain. These objectives are characterized by difficult access, complex route-finding, and numerous objective hazards.

This is primarily an early- to mid-spring zone. The steep southeast aspects will often begin the melt-freeze process in March. This also means they heat up rapidly and produce consequential wet snow avalanches in steep, confined terrain features. Time your descent early to avoid saturated surface snow. The south face of Ypsilon may hold a large, potentially hazardous cornice well into the spring.

Lawn Lake Trailhead is the main access to all 3 peaks. Enter the Park through the Fall River Entrance west of Estes Park. From the entrance station, follow Hwy 34 for 2.4 m. to a right turn (Old Fall River Road) and park at the first lot on the right.

For Chiquita, take the Ypsilon Lake Trail to Chipmunk Lake at ~10,600, climb Chiquita's east flank, and follow the ridge to the summit. **For Ypsilon and Fairchild**, continue on the Ypsilon Lake Trail to the lake. From here, the quickest way to the Ypsilon summit is via the slopes west of Donner Ridge. From the Lake, find the creek outlet on the west side, heading up into the basin between Ypsilon and Chiquita. Donner Ridge is Ypsilon's SE Ridge, above you to climbers' right. Continue west, above timberline, until you're under a steep, south-facing slope that climbs towards Ypsilon's summit. Spectacle Lakes are also accessed from Ypsilon Lake, via the west side of their outlet creek. For Fairchild, get to the NE corner of Ypsilon Lake and head north to Fay Lakes. To minimize bushwacking, use the steep gully just north of the lake to access a traversing bench.

From the bottom of the Banana Peel Couloir, staying on the north side of the creek to a 10,600' bench allows a rising traverse to the east/northeast. Hit the ridge at ~11,500' and move east back to the Ypsilon Lake trail. For all other routes, return to the Lawn Lake Trailhead via the Ypsilon Lake Trail.

1 MOUNT CHIQUITA–BANANA PEEL COULOIR 45° 2,000'

Tired of the crowds at Emerald Lake? Check out this steep, south-facing couloir on Mount Chiquita. It takes a bit of work to get in (and out), but you're unlikely to be fighting crowds. Take the Ypsilon Lake trail to Chipmunk Lake at ~10,600' and climb the east flank/ridge of Chiquita to the summit. Descend the continuous, south-facing couloir for 2,000' of sustained 40° turns. The line can be scoped from Hidden Valley and from multiple spots on Highway 34, making the top-down approach reasonable. To exit, stay on the north side of Chiquita Creek until a bench at 10,600' allows a rising traverse east/northeast. Hit the ridge at ~11,500 and keep trucking east back to the Ypsilon Lake Trail. This avoids difficult bushwhacking in the lower Chiquita Creek drainage. Plan for some skis-off time.

2 YPSILON MOUNTAIN–Y COULOIR 55° 2,500'

This challenging, dangerous route beckons intrepid ski mountaineers anytime they stare up at Ypsilon from Highway 34. Descents of this line are rare and should be carefully considered both for snowpack stability, access, and snow quality. A top-down approach avoids prolonged exposure to the cornice hazard overhead, as well as the challenge of climbing the WI4 pitch in the lower choke. From the summit, find (or build) an anchor in the talus blocks to rappel ~20m into the couloir, skiers' left of the cornice. Make steep, exhilarating turns to the obvious choke several hundred feet below. Approach the anchor (two pitons on skiers' right wall), make an exposed move to clip in, breath a sigh of relief, and rappel ~40m over the chimney (skis off recommended). Enjoy the turns down the apron below to Spectacle Lake. The length of the rappel may vary based on seasonal conditions, but plan on at least 35m to get below the water ice. Two 60m ropes is the safest bet. Due to the uncertain time intervals between descents, bring anchor material.

2 **Y COULOIR** *(see previous page)*

3 **Y LEFT** △ 55° ▽ 2,500'

The Y-Couloir's neighbor is only slightly less severe in slope angle, and lacking the mid-route rock band. No mandatory rappels. Approach Y Left directly from Spectacle Lake. In a typical season, there is cornice hazard overhead. Skin up the apron from the lake until boots are warranted. Split off to climbers' left at the obvious bifurcation and climb the curving couloir to an exit around the cornice, or descend from just below it.

4 **CUMBRE COULOIR** △ 50° ▽ 2,500'

A modern, aesthetic line first skied by Mark Kelly in Spring 2011, the Cumbre descends from the summit down the east face couloir of Ypsilon into the Fay Lakes drainage. A 30m rappel may be required to bypass unskiable ice in the choke. The anchor will likely need to be replaced. This section has also been downclimbed with crampons and a single ice ax. Exit by contouring back to Ypsilon Lake.

Fairchild Mountain

Ypsilon Lake

5 FAIRCHILD MOUNTAIN–SOUTH FACE   40°   2,500'
The most attainable summit ski line of the group, this one also has the
longest approach and a finicky exit ice bulge in the late season. Climb and ski
the obvious south-facing gully above Fay Lakes. The angle approaches 40° in
several spots. In the late season, several low-angled ice cascades and rock
ledges are exposed at the bottom of the route. They are generally simple to
traverse around. Return via your route of ascent.

See previous pages for:
2 Y COULOIR
3 Y LEFT
4 CUMBRE COULOIR

Big Basin *(p. 22)*

Upper Main

Trail Ridge Road

Columbine Trail

HIDDEN VALLEY OVERVIEW

An operational ski area from 1955–1991, Hidden Valley has been frequented by skiers since at least the 1930s, when National Park Service ski shuttles carried truckloads of people up Trail Ridge Road for a run back to the valley bottom. Its 2,000' vertical drop was ultimately served by 2 T-bars, 2 Poma lifts, and a double chair, with a base lodge for guests. These days, Hidden Valley is frequented by Park visitors with sleds, snowshoes, and skis. It offers easy access to moderate ski touring terrain both below and above timberline. In recent years, the NPS has provided an avalanche transceiver practice area near the base to climbers' right as you head up Columbine. Given the popularity of this terrain for ski tourers and other recreationists, please be considerate in setting your skintrack to both encourage repeated use and to preserve untracked snow for others. Also, if you choose to dig a snow pit, please locate it off the main thoroughfare and fill it back in to avoid creating a hazard for other travelers.

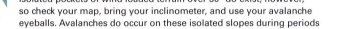

The vast majority of Hidden Valley is out of avalanche terrain. Isolated pockets of wind loaded terrain over 30° do exist, however, so check your map, bring your inclinometer, and use your avalanche eyeballs. Avalanches do occur on these isolated slopes during periods of high danger.

Hidden Valley is accessed primarily from the Hidden Valley Snow Play Area, located just downhill of the Many Parks Curve winter road closure. A large, plowed parking area also provides heated restrooms and a warming hut. Park at Many Parks Curve for a flat nordic ski tour on Trail Ridge Road.

Follow the Columbine Trail (see next page) up to Trail Ridge Road to gain the Upper Main Slope, or use the Aspen Trail (see next page) to climb up towards Big Basin.

Follow any of the listed runs back to the trailhead parking. Beware that venturing off well-used trails and into the trees can result in significant deadfall encounters.

*Green does not mean it's "easy." Green means "simple avalanche terrain." **Simple terrain definition**: Exposure to low-angle or primarily forested terrain. Some forest openings may involve the runout zones of infrequent avalanches. Many options to reduce or eliminate exposure. No glacier travel. Learn more about the ATES scale on page 7.*

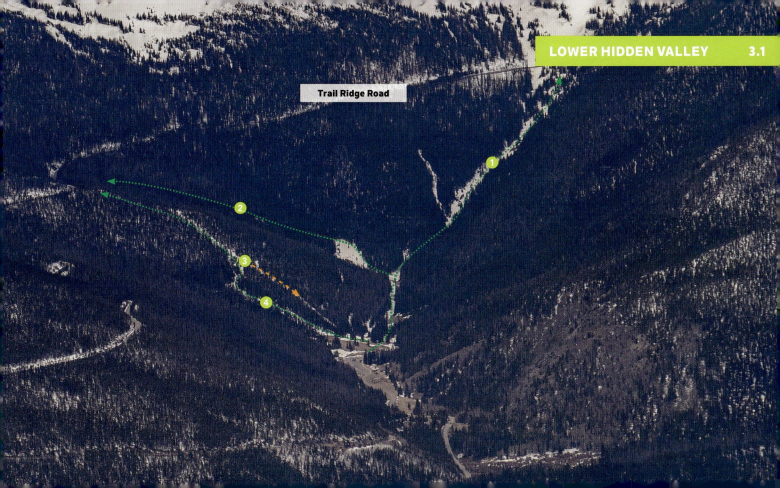

Trail Ridge Road

LOWER HIDDEN VALLEY

"The Lowers" includes any terrain below Trail Ridge Road, including Columbine, Aspen, Lift Line, and Spruce runs. Although many more ski runs were cut in the past, most have grown over to the point of being unskiable. The runs listed below are still reasonably clear and provide nice ascent routes or mellow turns below timberline.

The vast majority of Hidden Valley is out of avalanche terrain. Isolated pockets of wind loaded terrain over 30° do exist, however, so check your map, bring your inclinometer, and use your avalanche eyeballs. Avalanches do occur on these isolated slopes during periods of high danger.

Hidden Valley is accessed primarily from the Hidden Valley Snow Play Area, located just downhill of the Many Parks Curve winter road closure. A large, plowed parking area also provides heated restrooms and a warming hut. Park at Many Parks Curve for a flat nordic ski tour on Trail Ridge Road.

Follow the Columbine Trail to Trail Ridge Road, or use the Aspen Trail to access Lift Line and Spruce.

Follow any of the listed runs back to the trailhead parking. Beware that venturing off well-used trails and into the trees can result in significant deadfall encounters.

1 COLUMBINE 25° 1,000'

From the parking lot, follow the Hidden Valley Creek drainage west, up to Trail Ridge Road. This is the widely-used route to access the upper runs. The bottom portion stays flat and fairly narrow. Be careful of exiting skiers.

2 ASPEN 25° 1,000'

Aspen is a great zone to practice skinning and transitions, and serves as a good ascent route towards Big Basin. Begin on Columbine and travel .25 miles west to its intersection on the climbers' left.

3 LIFT LINE 30° 900'

This was the site of the Lower T-Bar. It is best used as a descent due to its narrow width.

4 SPRUCE 30° 900'

The farthest east run that hasn't been entirely grown in. Go to the bottom of Lift Line (allowing a wide berth for the sledding hill) and begin climbing behind the wood fence. This joins up with Lift Line after a few hundred feet.

Trail Ridge Road

EXIT

UPPER HIDDEN VALLEY

The Upper Bowl includes the Windows, Main, Upper Main, and Big Basin runs and is the most popular and accessible above timberline ski terrain in RMNP. It's a great area to quietly practice your craft, or to enjoy celebrating a pow day with half of the Front Range. There are plenty of options above Trail Ridge Road; go poke around!

 The vast majority of Hidden Valley is out of avalanche terrain. Isolated pockets of wind loaded terrain over 30° do exist, however, so check your map, bring your inclinometer, and use your avalanche eyeballs. Avalanches do occur on these isolated slopes during periods of high danger.

 Hidden Valley is accessed primarily from the Hidden Valley Snow Play Area, located just downhill of the Many Parks Curve winter road closure. A large, plowed parking area also provides heated restrooms and a warming hut. Park at Many Parks Curve for a flat nordic ski tour on Trail Ridge Road.

 Follow the Columbine Trail *(see next page)* up to Trail Ridge Road to gain the Upper Main Slope, or use the Aspen Trail (see next page) to climb up towards Big Basin.

 EXIT Follow any of the listed runs back to Lower Hidden Valley (previous page), then to the trailhead parking. Beware that venturing off well-used trails and into the trees can result in significant deadfall encounters.

❶ WINDOWS *(see next page)*　🔼 32°　🔽 1,000'
Windows is a partially treed run above Trail Ridge Road, just to the climbers' right of Upper Main. It can hold some protected snow when the Main runs are wind affected. Be cautious of the steeper terrain just north of Windows.

❷ UPPER MAIN *(see next page)*　🔼 30°　🔽 1,000'
Directly overhead when you intersect the road on Columbine. This offers a great fall line shot with plenty of options.

❸ MAIN　🔼 30°　🔽 1,000'
Further left of Upper Main is a collection of gullies, glades, and bowls that all lead back down to Trail Ridge Road.

❹ BIG BASIN　🔼 32°　🔽 1,000'
Head over here for some solitude, but realize that the approach will take a bit longer than the superhighway to Upper Main. Most folks follow Aspen up to the road, take a right, and follow the road until just under Big Basin. You're bound to encounter some deadfall above the road, but the route just east of the subtle drainage feature seems to have the least.

 Blue *does not mean this area is like a blue square run at the ski resort.* **Blue** *means "challenging avalanche terrain".*
Learn more about the ATES scale on p. 7.

EXIT

ONE GOOD _RIDE_ DESERVES ANOTHER

CRESTED BUTTE · GUNNISON VALLEY

Come bike **the backcountry.**

Hallett Peak

Flattop Mountain

Notchtop Mountain

Snowdrift Peak

1

2

3

Bear Lake

BEAR LAKE TRAILHEAD

The Bear Lake Trailhead provides the highest, most extensive access to wintertime ski touring and ski mountaineering terrain in the Park. Use this trailhead for access to Odessa Gorge, Tyndall Gorge, and Chaos Canyon ski tours. This trailhead is also an overflow parking option for routes in the Glacier Gorge sector, thanks to a 0.25-mile connecting trail between the two. This is a popular trailhead; in the heart of winter, expect it to fill up by mid-morning on weekends and holidays. Check the road status after winter storms to be sure it has been cleared by the NPS plows.

Given the diverse nature of the terrain configuration in this sector, expect any and all avalanche problems on your tour, in any of the three elevation bands.

After passing through the Beaver Meadows Entrance Station, take a left on Bear Lake Road and follow it 9.5 miles to its end. The trailhead has bathrooms, an emergency phone, and regular ranger hours. Winter access differs slightly from the summer trails in the Bear Lake vicinity. The lakes are usually frozen enough to cross from November to April. There are also a couple of direct options that follow winter-only trails, or creek drainages, described below.

Out-and-back tours are most common here, but one could access the south face of Flattop via Odessa Gorge. Take extra caution that you're not dropping in on Tyndall Gorge skiers when using this strategy.

❶ ODESSA GORGE APPROACH

To access Odessa Gorge and the north side of Flattop Mountain, head around the east edge of Bear Lake for 0.1 miles until you can split off right and onto the Bear Lake-Bierstadt Trail. Follow this for another 0.3 miles to a left turn onto the Flattop Mountain-Fern Lake Trail. Continue on this trail to access all ski tours on the north side of Flattop from the bottom up. The Flattop Mountain summer trail is not typically used for access to the Rock Garden or Banana Bowl.

❷ TYNDALL GORGE APPROACH

To access Dream Lake, find the winter use trail, which runs due west from the south side of Bear Lake, just behind the weather station. This will take you directly to Nymph Lake. Cross Nymph Lake to its southwest corner and continue west into the forest until you join back up with the summer trail at the east outlet of Dream Lake. From here, the Lake Haiyaha trail heads south and offers access to the Dream Chutes, Terrain Park, and Chaos Canyon tours. For upper Tyndall Gorge tours, continue west to Emerald Lake.

❸ CHAOS CANYON APPROACH

To get to Chaos Canyon, follow the approach to Dream Lake and the Lake Haiyaha Trail. Follow the trail past the Terrain Park entrance and descend to Lake Haiyaha.

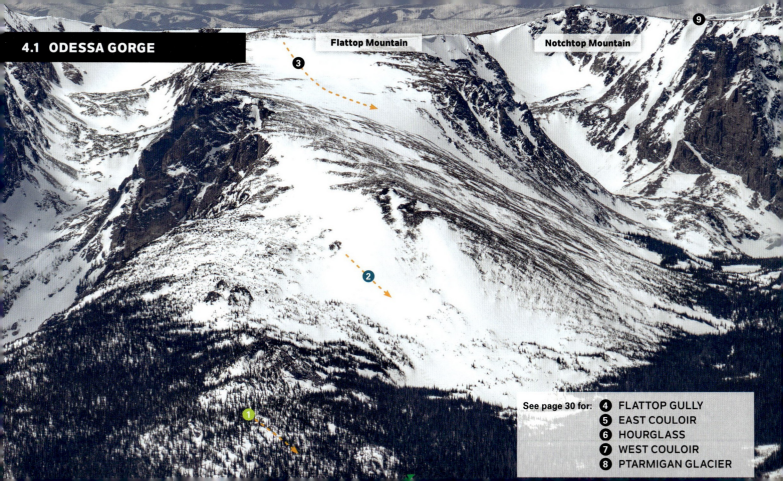

4.1 ODESSA GORGE

Flattop Mountain

Notchtop Mountain

See page 30 for:
4 FLATTOP GULLY
5 EAST COULOIR
6 HOURGLASS
7 WEST COULOIR
8 PTARMIGAN GLACIER

ATES 3

ODESSA GORGE

Odessa Gorge is the valley framed by the north side of Flattop Mountain and the south side of Notchtop Mountain. It offers skiing at all elevation bands and levels of difficulty, with fairly easy access from the Bear Lake Trailhead. Due to the shape and location of the drainage relative to the prevailing weather, expect amplification of wind speed here, especially above treeline.

See previous page for access, avy, approach, and exit info.

❶ ROCK GARDEN 35° 600'

This is a good place to score a few protected turns when the wind is howling above timberline. Ascend from the Fern Lake trail using openings in the tree coverage. Micro terrain above 30° exists, but the vast majority is lower-angle. Options exist to continue descending below the trail for a handful of extra turns. The name exists for a reason - watch out for shallow buried rocks!

❷ BANANA BOWL 30° 1,000'

This wide-open, northeast-facing bowl is a great place to come for a few laps when the weather is good enough to get up high, but the avalanche danger requires you to keep the slope angle low. When the Fern Lake Trail breaks out of the trees, head up and left to the obvious open slope. The skintrack usually goes up the climbers' right side. Descend the bowl, or check out the gullies and glades to skiers' right.

❸ FLATTOP NORTH FACE 35° 1,500'

The next slope past the Banana Bowl on the south side of the drainage. This is a great summit ski from Flattop when it's fully covered. Climb directly up it, starting from the east edge of Two Rivers Lake. Once atop the gully, head west towards the summit of Flattop on a mellow, open slope. Reverse your ascent route.

❹ FLATTOP GULLY 50° 1,200'

This is the serpentine couloir that descends from the west edge of Flattop's north face. It's a serious line with steep turns above exposure and a penchant for producing pockets of wind slab. Climb the route to assess conditions, or consider using a belay to ski-cut the entrance. Drop into the steep face along its east edge and funnel into a couloir that snakes left

and then back right before emptying out below the Ptarmigan Fingers. There may be an exposed rock band at the dogleg in the middle, requiring a short downclimb of moderate difficulty.

The following three runs are known as the Ptarmigan Fingers. They're all steep and leeward, dropping directly off of the Continental Divide. Large cornices and windslab potential exist. It's not uncommon to see broken ice on the upper tarn from avalanche debris.

❺ EAST COULOIR 50° 1,200'

This is the straight-as-an-arrow couloir that drops directly to the tarn.

❻ HOURGLASS   50° 1,200'

The middle feature that empties down onto the moraine bench.

❼ WEST COULOIR 50° 1,200'

The lookers' right couloir.

❽ PTARMIGAN GLACIER 30-45° 1,000'

The moderate bowl just north of the Ptarmigan Fingers. The climbers' left edge stays at or just above 30° and gets steeper as you look right.

❾ NOTCHTOP COULOIR 40° 1,200'

A Park classic. Climb directly above the upper tarn to the north and follow the long, consistent south-facing couloir to the top, trending right to avoid the cornice.

Hallett Peak

Bear Lake

ATES 3

TYNDALL GORGE

Tyndall Gorge serves as a main artery for ski tours in the Bear Lake zone. The North Buttress of Hallett Peak and South Face of Flattop Mountain provide a beautiful backdrop for intermediate and expert ski tours. This is a popular destination for winter backcountry enthusiasts, including hikers and snowshoers. Please be considerate when using the hiking trails and slow down or yield for uphill travelers.

Given the diverse nature of the terrain, expect any and all avalanche problems on your tour, in any of the three elevation bands.

Access and approach: See p. 27 for directions to Bear Lake Trailhead and approach instructions into Tyndall Gorge.

EXIT

Upper Tyndall Gorge tours all funnel back to Emerald or Dream Lakes. Return to the Bear Lake Trailhead via the hiking trail. For the Terrain Park, your return will be to the west edge of Nymph Lake via a traverse to the north at ~9,600'. This can be done without reapplying skins, but will require some sidestepping.

1 TYNDALL GLACIER  40° ▽ 2,200'

This long, winding, mostly moderate route follows the Tyndall Gorge all the way from Emerald Lake to the Continental Divide. It is best skied in spring, when heavier snowfall covers the talus boulders under Hallett Peak. Climb west from Emerald Lake, passing under Hallett's huge North Buttress. Find the path of least resistance through the moraines until you're underneath the Tyndall Glacier Headwall. Don your spikes and choose a route to the Divide. Options range from 40° up the middle of the bowl to 50° along the edges. Descend your ascent route.

2 TERRAIN PARK ◣ 35° ▽ 700'

The Terrain Park provides a short, east-facing descent from the Lake Haiyaha Trail down to Nymph Lake. Scope it from here on your way up, as several large cliff bands complicate the route finding. Rip your skins at 10,200', where the trail wraps around to a small concave bowl. Ski several short pitches, trending left, to an exit at the bottom of a talus field. Locate the return track at ~9,600' and take a left, crossing Tyndall Creek on your way back to Nymph Lake. Several variations exist for descent options; just get a lay of the land first.

3 DREAM CHUTES ◣ 40° ▽ 800'

The Dream Chutes are steep, north-facing tree runs that descend directly to the south and west edges of Dream Lake. Again, micro route-finding can be challenging and many variations exist. Even small wind or storm slabs can have consequences in this terrain. Follow the Lake Haiyaha trail past the Terrain Park entrance to a small saddle. The trail begins to descend southwest here towards the lake. Climb west from the saddle through the talus field to the ridge top. The feature is locally known as the Dream Dome. Traverse the ridge west, which may require a couple of skis-off sections. The first descent option you'll arrive at is the Center/Main Dream Chute. It begins at a small bowl that drops down and skier's right under a cliff band. The next pitch descends the fall line to Dream Lake. For the Leftist, continue west along the ridge to another short bowl that drops into the trees. Several options exist, but all should lead you to a short, steep gully that descends to the west edge of the lake.

4 HALLETT NORTH COULOIR *(see next pages)*
5 DRAGONTAIL COULOIR *(see next pages)*
6 DEAD ELK COULOIR *(see next pages)*
7 CORRAL COULOIR *(see next pages)*

Dream Lake

Bear Lake

② **TERRAIN PARK** *(see previous page for description)*

③ **DREAM CHUTES** *(see previous page for description)*

④ **HALLETT NORTH COULOIR**   45°   1,000'

In the springtime, this line often fills in to adequately cover the talus and provide a steep, continuous descent to Emerald Lake. From the west edge of Emerald Lake, climb the Tyndall Creek drainage to directly underneath the North Buttress of Hallett. Head left and transition to boots once the couloir steepens. This line is usually cornice-free. Descend your ascent route.

Dragontail Spire

❺ DRAGONTAIL COULOIR

▸ 55° ▾ 1,800'

Several steep, narrow couloirs descend the south face of Flattop Mountain to Emerald Lake. The Dragontail takes a direct line from the lake to the right of Dragontail Spire, where it splits into two branches for the top several hundred feet. Above the split, the climbers' left (west) branch is narrower and has less continuous snow cover towards the top. The climbers' right branch beckons with a wider crux and better snow coverage. However, the entrance is guarded by a large cornice and gets early and intense sun. Approach the right branch with extra caution. The most common way to approach and ride the Dragontail is from the bottom up, via Emerald Lake. If you choose to go top-down on it from Odessa Gorge, please be mindful of climbers below you on this popular route. Loose snow, wind, and storm slabs are common on this line, depending on recent conditions. They are often large enough to reach the west shore of Emerald Lake and cover the edge of the approach apron.

❻ DEAD ELK COULOIR

▸ 45° ▾ 1,800'

Immediately left of Dragontail is a parallel couloir that drops directly to Emerald Lake. The Dead Elk is slightly less steep, but has a rock band about two-thirds of the way up that is rarely covered. The climbing through the rock band is moderate, and often requires a short rappel on the descent. A slung boulder is usually in situ, but bring your own anchoring material if you plan to climb above this rock band.

❼ CORRAL COULOIR

▸ 45° ▾ 800'

The couloir is named after the horse corral located at the top of the line, along the Flattop Mountain Trail. It is often skied top-down and used as a connector between the Odessa and Tyndall drainages. Access it via the Banana Bowl and Flattop Mountain Trail, or tack it onto an upper Tyndall Gorge tour. It reliably forms a huge cornice along its west edge, and is often peppered with talus in the lower half. Join up with the Tyndall Glacier route and descend to Emerald Lake.

Otis Peak

Hallett Peak

Lake Haiyaha

CHAOS CANYON

Chaos Canyon is framed by Hallett Peak to the north and Otis Peak to the south. It is named for the number of erratic boulders that litter the valley, sometimes making it difficult to navigate. Its centerpiece is Lake Haiyaha, which is surrounded by ski touring options from mellow glades to steep couloirs.

Chaos Canyon includes terrain with multiple aspects and elevations. All avalanche types can occur, depending on terrain and conditions.

See page 27 for directions to Bear Lake Trailhead and approach instructions into Tyndall Gorge.

Options include: Exit via Mario Gully and return to Nymph Lake. Climb back up to the Terrain Park and return to Nymph Lake. From Lake Haiyaha, climb north to the Dream Chutes and return via Dream Lake

① MARIO GULLY *(see next page)* 35° 500'

Mario Gully follows the Chaos Creek drainage to its intersection with Tyndall Creek. Depending on snow coverage, it may provide a continuous descent with some entertaining boulder pillows, but beware of open water in the drainage itself. The skiers' left flank provides the best ski terrain otherwise. At the bottom of the gully, traverse left to join the Terrain Park return route to Nymph Lake.

② OTIS COULOIRS *(see next page)* 45° 500'

These twin couloirs drop north from the east shoulder of Otis Peak into the south edge of the Chaos drainage. They can be approached bottom-up, but are most commonly accessed via The Loch's east edge. "The Otis Tour" starts from Bear Lake parking lot (with skins in your pack!) and descends the Bear Lake-Glacier Gorge trail to join the Loch Vale approach. From The Loch, climb up the backside of the Otis Couloirs and descend into Chaos Creek. Take a lap in the Easy Alleys, and return to the Tyndall drainage via route of your choice.

③ EASY ALLEYS *(AKA Otis Glades)* 30° 400'

These short, mellow shots are located just above the south side of Lake Haiyaha. Combined with a Terrain Park exit, they make a great midwinter tour of the area. Approach by skiing across Haiyaha to its west side and wrap around south, avoiding the large boulders along the lake's edge. A lap track can be put in on the west side of the run.

④ CHAOS COULOIR *(see p. 39)* 45° 700'

This south-facing line descends from Hallett's East Ridge to the northwest corner of Lake Haiyaha. It is most commonly approached by skinning from the lake until it's too steep and narrow, then booting the top to the ridge.

⑤ ELEVATOR SHAFT *(see p. 39)* 55° 1,500'

Another classic steep, south-facing couloir drops from the upper east ridge of Hallett into Chaos Creek. Approach this line from Lake Haiyaha. The crux is in the top section of the couloir.

⑥ HALLETT PEAK SOUTH FACE *(see p. 39)* 40° 2,500'

In June of 2022, a massive spontaneous rockfall occurred on this line and obliterated the middle section of the route. This description is provided to inform the reader of the historical route, but should be interpreted with knowledge that the newly established line could differ significantly.
The South Face of Hallett has long been a classic summit descent into the Chaos drainage. Gain the summit of Hallett Peak via Chaos, Tyndall, or Flattop's summit. Descend the ridge to the east until clear of the massive cornice that hangs over the southeast face and ski the fall line into upper Chaos. Continue via the path of least resistance (often skiers' left) to Lake Haiyaha.

Hallett North Couloir
(p. 34)

① MARIO GULLY *(see p. 37)*   35°   500'
② OTIS COULOIRS *(see p. 37)*   45°   500'
③ EASY ALLEYS *(see p. 37)*   30°   400'

6 Hallett Peak

Flattop Mountain

5

4

Lake Haiyaha

4	CHAOS COULOIR *(see p. 37)*	45°	700'
5	ELEVATOR SHAFT *(see p. 37)*	55°	1,500'
6	HALLETT PEAK SOUTH FACE	40°	2,500'
	(see p. 37 for descriptions and special hazard info)		

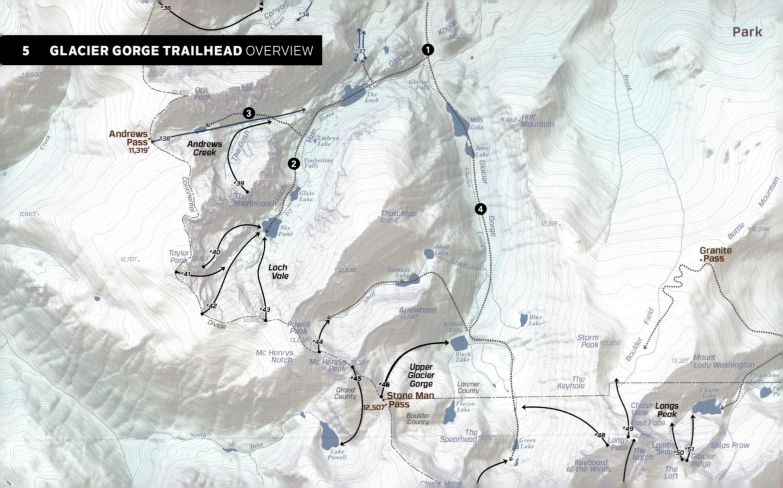

Park

Canyon
Chaos
#36
#34

#37

Otis
Peak
12,486' 12,482'
11,932'

Glacier
Glacier
Falls
Knobe
11,085'
①

The Loch
Mills
Lake
11,482'
Half
Mountain

③
#38
The Gash
Brook
Vale
Embryo
Lake
Forel
Lake

Andrews
Pass
11,319'
Andrews
Creek

Continental

②
Timberline
Falls

Glacier
Glacier
Gorge

④
12,158'
11,663'
#39
12,630'
The
Sharkstooth

Glass
Lake
Thatchtop
12,668'

Icy

Sky
Pond

Shelf
Lake

Granite
Pass

Battle Mountain
12,044'

Taylor
Peak
12,701'
#40
#50'

Loch
Vale

Solitude
Lake

Arrowhead
12,387'

Blue
Lake

Storm
Peak
13,326'

Boulder Field

Mount
Lady
Washington
13,321'

#41
11,936'

12,836'

#42
13,015'
#43
Divide

Powell
Peak
13,208'

Shelf

Ribbon
Falls

Black
Lake

The
Keyhole

Chasm View
East Face
13,223'

#44

McHenrys
Notch

McHenrys
Peak
13,327'

Larimer
County

Chasm Lake

Mount
Meeker
13,911'

#45

Grand
County

#46
Stone Man
Pass
12,507'

Upper
Glacier
Gorge

Frozen
Lake

Boulder
County

The
Spearhead
12,575'

Green
Lake

#48
Longs
Peak

Longs
Peak
14,259'
#49

Chasm
View

The
Notch

Lambs
Slide
#50

Columbine
#51
Glacier
Ridge

Ships Prow

North
Inlet

Lake
Powell

Keyboard
of the Winds

The
Loft

Christe's Ma..

GLACIER GORGE TRAILHEAD OVERVIEW

The Glacier Gorge Trailhead offers year-round access to Loch Vale, Andrews Creek, Solitude Lake, and upper Glacier Gorge itineraries.

Given the diversity of the terrain in this sector, expect any and all avalanche problems on your tour, in any of the three elevation bands.

To reach the parking area, go through the Beaver Meadows Entrance Station and take a left onto Bear Lake Road. Continue for 8.5 miles to the parking lot on the left. This lot only has spaces for a couple dozen vehicles and it fills quickly. An alternative is to continue up the road to the larger Bear Lake Trailhead and ski south (downhill) for 0.4 miles on the Bear Lake-Glacier Gorge connector trail to its intersection with Chaos Creek. Skins on from here as you join the standard Glacier Gorge approach.

All itineraries lead back to the Glacier Gorge or Loch Vale trails. Exit as you approached.

1 **Approach to Loch Vale-Glacier Gorge Junction:** From the trailhead parking, head west on the Glacier Gorge Trail for 0.4 miles to an intersection with the Bear Lake-Glacier Gorge Trail. Take a left and head south for another 0.15 miles to an unmarked right turn onto the winter trail that follows a drainage on the north side of the Glacier Knobs. This route often has enough coverage for skiing from December to May, and will take you directly to the Glacier Gorge-Loch Vale Junction.

2 **Loch Vale Approach:** From the junction, stay on the Glacier Gorge Trail for 0.1 miles to its first creek crossing (bridge). Climbing west up this drainage (Icy Brook) is the preferred winter route. Follow the creek bed for 0.5 miles to The Loch. Cross it and pick up the Sky Pond Trail on the west side. This point can also be reached via the Loch Vale hiking trail if the creek bed is open and running.

3 **Andrews Approach:** From The Loch, another 0.4 miles will take you to the Andrews Creek intersection on the right. If the bridge and sign are covered with snow, this is easy to miss. Follow the approximate path of the summer trail to treeline, where a turn to the west will have you heading up towards the Divide.

4 **Upper Glacier Gorge Approach:** From the Glacier Gorge-Loch Vale Junction, follow the Glacier Gorge Trail. Ski across Mills and Jewel Lakes. From the south edge of Jewel Lake, take the time to locate the trail, as a blowdown has made off-trail travel very difficult between here and Black Lake. Later in the season, it's possible to follow Glacier Creek directly for much of this section. Total distance from the junction to Black Lake: 2.5 miles. From Black Lake, the route heads east up a low-angle gully to access the upper bench. When coverage and conditions allow, it is possible to ascend the avalanche path west of Black Lake directly towards McHenrys Peak and Stoneman Pass.

Taylor Peak

Otis Peak

Mills Lake

The Loch

Loch-GG Junction

Glacier Gorge

LOCH VALE

ATES 3

Loch Vale is a dramatic cirque that provides classic steep skiing—almost entirely above timberline and in expert terrain. Conditions often come into shape here in March and good snow coverage can last well into May.

The terrain is steep and almost entirely leeward to the Continental Divide. It regularly produces both loose snow and slab avalanches through the winter and into the early summer. Cornices threaten all of the routes above Sky Pond.

See previous page for directions to Glacier Gorge Trailhead and approach instructions to the Glacier Gorge-Loch Vale Junction.

From The Loch, another 0.4 miles will take you to the Andrews Creek intersection, and 0.5 miles more will have you cresting Timberline Falls into upper Loch Vale.

EXIT

These are all out-and-back tours.

Black does not mean this area is like a black diamond run at the ski resort. Black means "complex avalanche terrain". Learn more about the ATES scale on page 7.

❶ POWELL PEAK NORTH FACE 50° ▼ 2,000′

This steep, sustained snowfield is south of Sky Pond and offers a clean, challenging descent. Several options exist for topping out; some have cornices.

❷ TAYLOR HEADWALL AKA SKY COULOIR 55° ▼ 2,000′

To the southwest of Sky Pond is Taylor Peak and the Taylor Glacier. The Sky Couloir is the plumb line on the lookers' right side of the prominent snowfield, narrowing as it climbs from the apron. Depending on the exact line, the angle could get even steeper and be capped by a cornice.

❸ TAYLOR SOUTHEAST COULOIR 45° ▼ 2,000′

This narrow hallway is hidden from view until you're right underneath it. Climb southwest from Sky Pond towards the Taylor Glacier. The line forms the boundary of Taylor Peak's south face and continues uninterrupted to the Divide.

❹ TAYLOR EAST FACE RAMP 40° ▼ 1,800′

Taylor Peak's East Face stands tall over Sky Pond. The East Face Ramp slashes across its midsection and provides a unique, surprisingly moderate ski descent. Access it from the north side of Sky Pond. Link snow between talus fields until you can turn skier's left to get on the ramp, which holds consistent snow coverage for much of the winter and spring. The terrain here is moderate, but consider overhead hazard when climbing under the steep East Face. Take the track to the top of the ramp and descend.

McHenrys Notch

Powell Peak

Sharks Tooth

Taylor Peak

Andrews Creek
(next page)

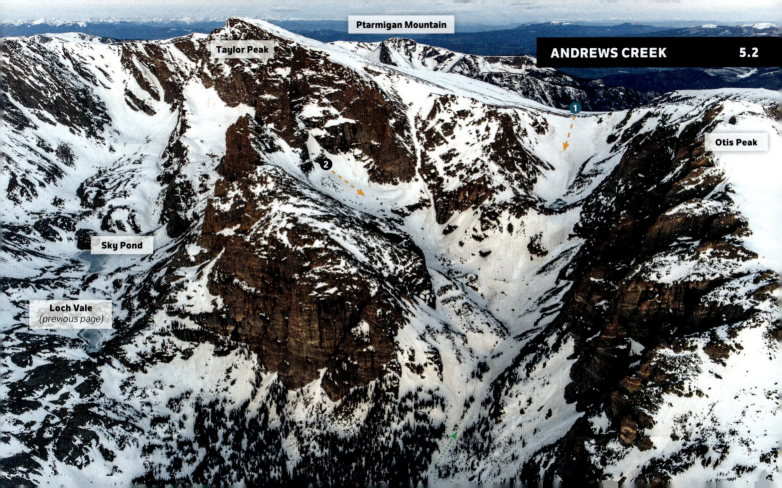

Ptarmigan Mountain

Taylor Peak

Otis Peak

Sky Pond

Loch Vale
(previous page)

ANDREWS CREEK

Andrews Creek splits from the Sky Pond Trail just west of The Loch and leads you to another world of glacier-carved cirques and dramatic towers.

The terrain is steep and almost entirely leeward to the Continental Divide. It regularly produces both loose snow and slab avalanches through the winter and into the early summer.

See beginning of chapter 5 for directions to Glacier Gorge Trailhead and approach instructions to the Glacier Gorge-Loch Vale Junction.

From The Loch, another 0.4 miles will take you to the Andrews Creek intersection on the right. If the bridge and sign are covered with snow, this is easy to miss. Follow the approximate path of the summer trail to treeline, where a turn to the west will have you heading up towards the Divide.

These are all out-and-back tours.

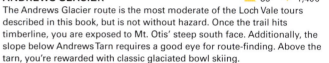

❶ ANDREWS GLACIER 35° 1,400'

The Andrews Glacier route is the most moderate of the Loch Vale tours described in this book, but is not without hazard. Once the trail hits timberline, you are exposed to Mt. Otis' steep south face. Additionally, the slope below Andrews Tarn requires a good eye for route-finding. Above the tarn, you're rewarded with classic glaciated bowl skiing.

❷ THE GASH 38° 1,500'

Access The Gash via Andrews Creek. Ascend the drainage as for Andrews Glacier to 10,800', then veer south towards the Sharkstooth (you'll know it). The approach is blocked by a cliff band at 11,200'. Breach it via a short couloir leading to a bench. Continue into the upper bowl to find many options for descent amongst the towers.

Black *does not mean this area is like a black diamond run at the ski resort.* **Black** *means "complex avalanche terrain". Learn more about the ATES scale on p. 7.*

Longs Peak

Chiefs Head

McHenrys Peak

Mills Lake

Loch Vale

UPPER GLACIER GORGE OVERVIEW

ATES 3

The Glacier Gorge Trailhead offers year-round access to Loch Vale, Andrews Creek, Solitude Lake, and upper Glacier Gorge itineraries.

See page 41 for directions to Glacier Gorge Trailhead, the Glacier Gorge-Loch Vale Junction, and to Upper Glacier Gorge descents.

Solitude Lake Approach: From the Loch Vale-Glacier Gorge Junction, continue on the Glacier Gorge Trail towards Black Lake. At 10,500', or just 0.1 miles north of Black Lake, cross Glacier Creek and begin ascending northwest through the forest, linking together ramps and gullies. You're aiming to get around the northeast ridge of Arrowhead Peak and hit the south side of Shelf Lake. This is a better approach on skis than the Shelf Lake summer trail. From here, continue to the upper drainage past Solitude Lake. Ski crampons can be helpful on this approach.

1 MCHENRYS NOTCH COULOIR 55° 1,200'

This secluded classic is worth the price of admission. Follow the approach to Solitude Lake and the upper Shelf Creek basin. Climb and descend the couloir. The crux is at the very top, but expect continuous 45° skiing through much of the couloir. This descent is best enjoyed in the early to mid-spring, when good snow coverage allows for continuous skinning up to Shelf Lake.

2 STONEMAN PASS 40° 1,900'

A great introduction to skiing in Glacier Gorge. Experience the vast, wide-open terrain of the upper basin when this route is in shape. From Black Lake, use the west side approach up the prominent avalanche path to gain the upper bench. Aim for the pass, which is on the east shoulder of McHenrys Peak, to the lookers' right of the "Stoneman." Switch to boots for the final couloir and descend your ascent route. You can also approach Stoneman Pass via the east side of Black Lake, which avoids the large avalanche path, but adds distance.

3 CHIEFS HEAD PEAK ROYAL RAMP COULOIR 50° 1,700'

Viewed from the valley, the Royal Ramp Couloir slashes across the northeast face of Chiefs Head, but does not reveal its terminus. The bottom does go clean and the lower ramp presents a steep, exposed crux over a large cliff. Although the couloir faces mostly north, the lower ramp and exit traverse turn east, so plan for an early sunhit. Approach via the east side of Black Lake and continue south across the upper basin to Green Lake. Climb a short gully to access the exposed snowfield traverse and continue up the prominent couloir to the ridge. Descend your ascent route.

4 MCHENRYS PEAK SOUTHEAST FACE 50° 1,700'

When conditions are right, this is the only non-technical ski route off the summit of McHenrys Peak. Climb to Stoneman Pass and choose a route up the East Ridge or directly up the Southeast Face to the summit. Descend towards Lake Powell, and reascend to Stoneman Pass to exit.

5 LONGS PEAK TROUGH 50° 2,500'

Although not a summit ski route on Longs Peak, the Trough provides great access to the upper mountain—and endless turns from the northwest shoulder of the peak—when it's filled in. Approach from the east side of Black Lake and continue south across the upper bench towards Green Lake. At 11,300', turn west and begin climbing the couloir. Due to its west aspect, continuous snow coverage usually only happens for a month or less, often in May.

McHenrys Peak

Apache Peak

Copeland Mountain

Chiefs Head Peak

Mount Alice

3

2

Shelf Lake

Black Lake

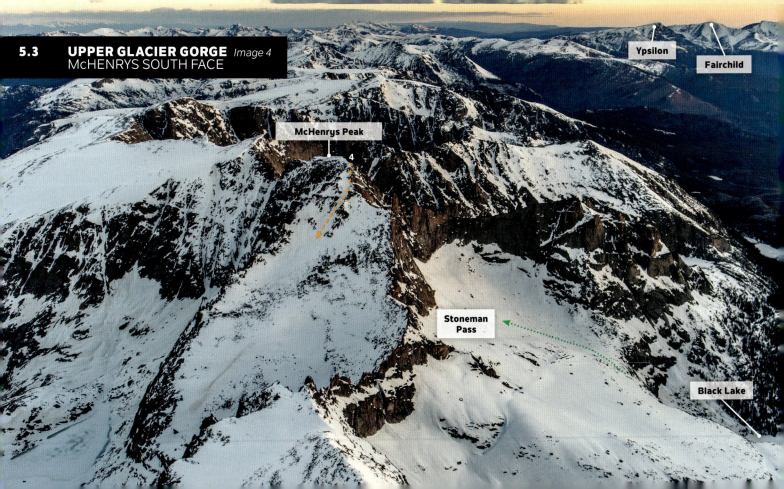

Ypsilon

Fairchild

McHenrys Peak

4

Stoneman Pass

Black Lake

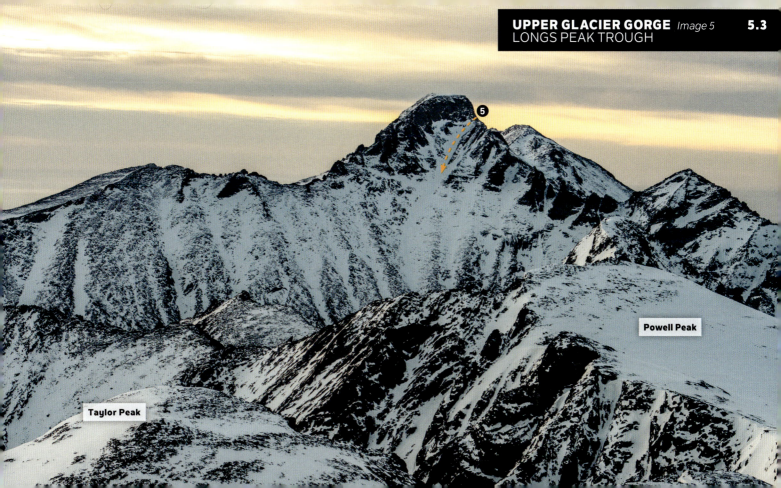

Powell Peak

Taylor Peak

The Loft

Chasm Lake

LONGS PEAK

The east side of Longs Peak is frequented by alpinists and rock climbers, but less often by ski mountaineers. Much of the peak is windswept and dry for most of the year, but each spring yields a short window for riding its high slopes. May to early June is the time to watch; keep an eye on the Longs Peak webcam to track coverage.

The east side of Longs Peak is popular with ski mountaineers in mid-to-late spring. Loose snow, storm slab, and wind slab avalanches are most common in this terrain throughout that time. During or immediately following storm events and periods of rapid warming are the most common times to see natural avalanche activity, which can threaten all of this complex terrain.

The Longs Peak Trailhead is off of Highway 7, 10 miles south of Estes Park and 25 miles west of Lyons. The trailhead has bathrooms and a ranger station. Unlike the Trail Ridge/Bear Lake corridor, there is no entrance station to collect a fee.

Chasm Lake Approach: From the trailhead, you will likely be walking on dirt or thin snow coverage. Bring running shoes and consider microspikes. Follow the Longs Peak Trail for just over 3 miles to Chasm Junction. From here, continue west on the Chasm Lake Trail towards the massive East Face of Longs for another 0.75 miles to Chasm Lake. Crossing the lake on skis is often the best option until mid-spring, when talus-hopping along its north shore is a safer bet. Cairns mark the best route.

North Face Approach: From the trailhead, you will likely be walking on dirt or thin snow coverage. Bring running shoes and consider microspikes. Follow the Longs Peak Trail for just over 3 miles to Chasm Junction. Take a right at the junction and head north on the East Longs Peak Trail, wrap around Mount Lady Washington, and arrive at the Boulderfield campsite, 2.5 miles from the junction.

These are out-and-back routes. Plan on switching back to hiking shoes at some point on the egress. Occasionally, skiable snow coverage will continue all the way to the trailhead.

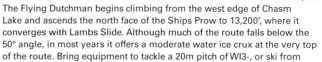

❶ FLYING DUTCHMAN COULOIR   50°   1,400'

The Flying Dutchman begins climbing from the west edge of Chasm Lake and ascends the north face of the Ships Prow to 13,200', where it converges with Lambs Slide. Although much of the route falls below the 50° angle, in most years it offers a moderate water ice crux at the very top of the route. Bring equipment to tackle a 20m pitch of WI3-, or ski from below the crux.

❷ LAMBS SLIDE COULOIR   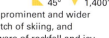 45°   1,400'

Lambs Slide is the next couloir to the west, more prominent and wider than the Dutchman. It offers a long, continuous pitch of skiing, and often sees ski tracks eight months of the year. Beware of rockfall and icy conditions in late summer and fall.

❸ LONGS PEAK NORTH FACE *(AKA Cables Route)*   50°   1,400'

The most direct, accessible Longs Peak summit descent. The Cables Route follows the hourglass-shaped wall above the Boulderfield campsite. It has all the makings of a classic extreme ski route: consistent angle, consequential exposure over the Diamond, and a brief technical challenge to get through the 5th-class rock section at the crux. The only drawbacks are that it's relatively short and has a brief window of skiable conditions, often in late May. From the Boulderfield, climb (on skis, if you're lucky) through the talus to Chasm View, which is the ridgetop perch at 13,500'. The crux is above you and can range from 5.4 rock climbing to a steep, snow-plastered slab. Climb one ~40m pitch using the eyebolts and a few midsize cams for protection. If the crux is not skiable, these eyebolts will be your rappel anchors on the descent; mark their location on the way up. The summit of Longs peak is a sizable plateau, and the fall line route takes you to the north end of it. Begin your descent here.

Chasm View

The Boulderfield

2

Longs Peak

❷

The Notch

Mt. Meeker

❶

ATES 3 LONGS + MEEKER SOUTH

The south/southwest faces of Longs and Mount Meeker rise out of Wild Basin for 3,000+ uninterrupted vertical feet. This places them near the top of the list for longest snow routes in the Front Range. Access is challenging and conditions are fickle. It's not uncommon for these lines to be completely dry in April, only to get filled in by a couple of May upslope storms.

 The springtime window for best conditions on these routes is fairly short. Considering their steepness and east-south exposure, wet snow avalanches are highest on the list of snowpack concerns for most attempts.

 From Estes Park, travel south on Highway 7 for 13.5 miles to the Wild Basin turnoff (CO Hwy 115). The Sandbeach Lake Trailhead is immediately on your right. The winter trailhead is another 1.3 miles up the road, where you will park at a locked gate. Sometime in May, this gate will open and allow travel for another mile to the summer trailhead and ranger station.

 Keplingers and Dragons Egg Approach:
For Dragons Egg: Begin at the Sandbeach Lake Trailhead. Follow the Sandbeach Lake Trail (often dry) for 3.5 miles to Hunters Creek. Turn right at Hunters Creek (primitive trail) and follow it for about 1 mile, where you can begin a climbing traverse into the gully.
For Keplingers: Begin at the Sandbeach Lake Trailhead. Follow it for about 5 miles, to a point 0.5 miles north of Sandbeach Lake, where you'll have to traverse along Hunters Creek to the base of the couloir.

 Follow your approach route back to the Sandbeach Lake Trailhead. It's worth sticking with the trail when possible, as off-trail navigation is notoriously brushy and difficult in this area.

❶ MOUNT MEEKER-DRAGONS EGG COULOIR 45° 3,200'

When conditions are right, this is the longest continuous vertical descent in RMNP. Look for it after May upslope storms plaster the east side of the Park; it can be scoped from Highway 7, north of Allenspark. From the Sandbeach Lake-Hunter Creek approach, climb the never-ending gully to the summit ridge of Meeker, passing the namesake boulder on your left. The route does not descend from the summit, which is a short rock scramble to the west. It is not uncommon to approach this route from the Longs Peak Trailhead, using either the Loft or the Dreamweaver Couloir. However, the Sandbeach Lake approach is quickest, doesn't rely on a vehicle shuttle, and allows you to scope the route as you climb.

❷ LONGS PEAK-KEPLINGERS COULOIR 45° 3,000'

Keplingers is the only reliably non-technical summit descent route on Longs Peak. It connects the Homestretch section with a long, southwest-facing couloir for an engaging 14er experience. As is par for the course, it usually comes into best condition from May to early June. Follow the approach past Sandbeach Lake, to the unnamed lake along Hunters Creek at 11,200'. Climb north up the winding couloir to ~13,600', where a rising traverse to skier's left will take you to the Homestretch section and the summit. There are several southwest-facing couloirs between Longs summit and the Loft. Identify Keplingers as the one that drops continuously from the Notch, along the south ridge.

Mt. Alice 1

Lion Lakes

LION LAKE

Mount Alice is a secluded wilderness gem, and the Rabbit Hole Couloir is a fine summit ski route worth a weekend trip.

The main avalanche concerns in this sector come from the steep northeast face of Mt Alice. Potential for both loose snow and slab avalanches exist on the approach slopes and in the couloir.

See previous page for directions to the Wild Basin Trailhead and approach instructions.

Lion Lake Approach from the Wild Basin Summer Trailhead:
Follow the Wild Basin Trail for 1.5 miles to a right turn on the Thunder Lake Trail. Another 2.6 miles will take you to the Lion Lake Trail intersection, follow this for 2.2 miles to Lion Lake #1. Bivy here or continue west towards the prominent east face of Mount Alice.

Return to the Wild Basin Trailhead

❶ NORTHEAST COULOIR *(AKA Rabbit Hole)*  50° 2,000'

From Lion Lake #1, climb west, towards the east face of Mount Alice. At 11,400', follow the drainage to the north to access the northeast basin and the couloir, which is the only weakness through the cliff bands. Climb the narrowing couloir to where it intersects with the upper snowfield and continue up moderate terrain to the summit.

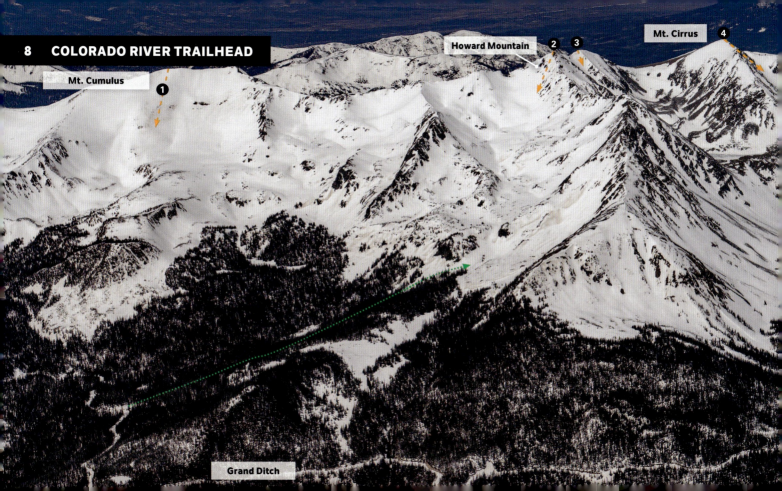

Mt. Cumulus

Howard Mountain

Mt. Cirrus

Grand Ditch

COLORADO RIVER TRAILHEAD

The west side of RMNP sees little winter visitation. Access and amenities are limited, and the town of Grand Lake focuses on ice fishing and snowmobiling as its main forms of recreation. If you don't mind making the long drive around the Divide, it's a great place to go ski touring. Expect a more adventurous outing. Late winter into mid-spring is the ideal time to catch these lines in condition, although there's still plenty of snow once Trail Ridge Road opens in late spring.

The Never Summer Mountains see slightly more snow and slightly less wind than the east side of the Park. During the winter, the snowpack is likely to have persistent slab and wind slab problems, which often evolve into storm snow and wet snow problems as the spring snowpack deepens and the weather warms.

From the town of Grand Lake, follow Highway 34 north for 1.5 miles to the Kawuneeche/Grand Lake Entrance Station. Continue for another 9.9 miles to the Colorado River Trailhead. This is also the winter closure for Trail Ridge Road on the west side of RMNP. This point can be reached from Estes Park after the road opens, usually around Memorial Day.

From the trailhead, travel northwest (behind the bathroom) and cross the Colorado River. Hold the same heading towards Opposition Creek, until you can intersect the Red Mountain Trail. Use this trail as your handrail to get to the Grand Ditch, aiming for an intersection point just south of Opposition Creek, ~10,250'. The Grand Ditch is a water diversion infrastructure that makes for an easy traverse route across the Never Summers.

Return to your ascent track along the Grand Ditch and follow it back to the trailhead.

❶ MOUNT CUMULUS EAST BOWL 35° 2,500'

From the intersection of Grand Ditch/Opposition Creek, follow the broad ridge just south of the creek to 10,600' and turn north, aiming for the east ridge of Cumulus. Continue near the ridge, following the path of least resistance to the summit. Ski the large bowl dropping east and work your way back south to Opposition Creek and the Ditch.

❷ HOWARD MOUNTAIN SOUTHEAST FACE 40° 2,600'

Travel north along the Ditch to Mosquito Creek and ascend along its east (looker's right) side to 10,800'. Surmount a short step to Pinnacle Pool and head west into the upper basin at 11,400'. Gain the ridge just south of Howard's summit and continue to the top. The Southeast Face route drops back into your ascent route directly from the summit.

❸ HOWARD MOUNTAIN NORTHEAST COULOIR   45° 2,600'

Use the Southeast Face approach route to the summit. There are several descent options dropping northeast to Lake of the Clouds. The most prominent begins on the ridge just northwest of the summit. From the lake, stay on the north side of Big Dutch Creek and the Lake of the Clouds Trail, leading to the Ditch.

❹ MOUNT CIRRUS NORTHEAST FACE   45° 2,600'

This is best tacked onto the Howard Northeast descent. Ascend west from the Lake of the Clouds to the ridge south of Cirrus' summit. Descend the prominent gully northeast off the summit and wrap around east to join the Lake of the Clouds Trail back to the Ditch.

Mt. Cumulus

Opposition Creek

Grand Ditch

EXIT

Howard Mountain

Mt. Cirrus

2

3

4

Grand Ditch

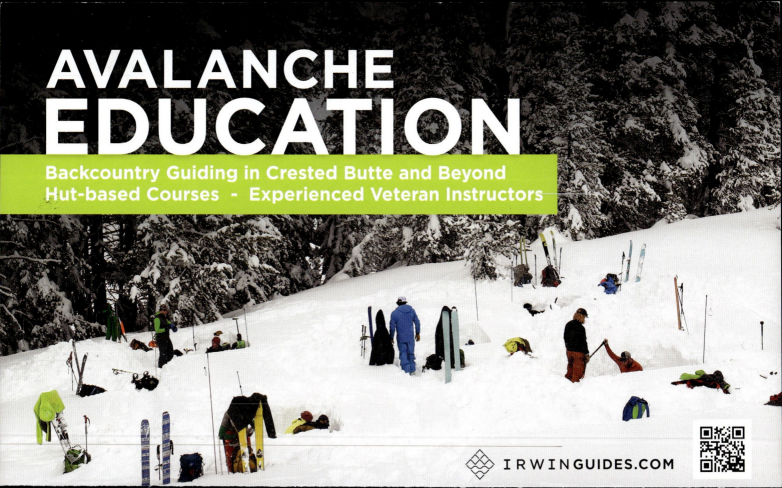

AVALANCHE EDUCATION

Backcountry Guiding in Crested Butte and Beyond
Hut-based Courses - Experienced Veteran Instructors

IRWINGUIDES.COM